3-98

Traditional Crafts from
MEXICO AND CENTRAL AMERICA

Traditional Crafts from
MEXICO AND CENTRAL AMERICA

by Florence Temko

with illustrations by Randall Gooch
and photographs by Robert L. and Diane Wolfe

Lerner Publications Company • Minneapolis

To David, Perri, Rachel, Linda, and Ronald

Over the years, I have tucked away bits of information in my files that have contributed to my fascination with crafts. They were gathered mainly from personal meetings, books, magazines, libraries, and museums. I regret it is no longer possible to disentangle these many and varied resources, but I would like to acknowledge gratefully and humbly everyone who has helped to make this book possible. —Florence Temko

Text copyright © 1996 by Florence Temko
Illustrations copyright © 1996 by Lerner Publications Company

Library of Congress Cataloging-in-Publication Data

Temko, Florence.
   Traditional crafts from Mexico and Central America / by Florence Temko ; illustrated by Randall Gooch ; photographs by Robert L. and Diane Wolfe.
     p. cm.—(Culture crafts)
   Includes index.
   Summary: Provides instructions on how to make traditional Mexican and Central American handicraft such as metal ornaments, tissue paper banners, and Guatemalan worry dolls.
   ISBN 0-8225-2935-1 (alk. paper)
   1. Handicraft—Mexico—Juvenile literature. 2. Handicraft—Central America— Juvenile literature. [1. Handicraft—Mexico. 2. Handicraft—Central America.] I. Title. II. Series.
TT28.T46 1996
745.5—dc20   95-46583

Manufactured in the United States of America
1 2 3 4 5 6 – JR – 01 00 99 98 97 96

CONTENTS

WHAT ARE CRAFTS?

All over the world, people need baskets, bowls, clothes, and tools. People now make many of these things in factories. But long ago, people made what they needed by hand. They formed clay and metal pots for cooking. They wove cloth to wear. They made baskets to carry food. We call these things "crafts" when they are made by hand.

Grandparents and parents taught children how to make crafts. While they worked, the elders told stories. These stories told of their family's culture—all of the ideas and customs that a group of people believe in and practice. Children learned these stories as they learned the ways of making crafts. They painted or carved symbols from those stories on their crafts.

Year after year, methods and symbols were passed from parents to children. Still, each bowl or basket they made would look a little different. A craft made by hand—even by the same person—never turns out the exact same way twice.

People who are very good at making crafts are called artisans. Many artisans still use the old methods. They make useful things for themselves and their homes. Some artisans also sell their crafts to earn money.

Left to right: A painted tile from Turkey, a Pueblo Indian pitcher, a pot from Peru, and a porcelain dish from China

MATERIALS AND SUPPLIES

Some of the suggested materials for the crafts in this book are the same as those used by Mexican and Central American artisans. Others will give you almost the same results. Most materials can be found at home or purchased at local stores. Check your telephone book for stores in your area that sell art materials, craft supplies, and teachers' supplies. Whenever you can, try to use recyclable materials—and remember to reuse or recycle the scraps from your projects.

MEASUREMENTS

Sizes are given in inches. If you prefer to use the metric system, you can use the conversion chart on page 58. Because fractions can be hard to work with, round all metric measurements to the nearest whole number.

FINISHES

The crafts in this book that are made from paper will last longer if you brush or sponge them with a thin coat of finish. These are some choices:

White glue (Elmer's or another brand) is the most widely available. Use it at full strength or dilute it with a few drops of water. Apply it with a brush or small sponge. (The sponge should be thrown away after you use it.) White glue dries clear.

Acrylic medium is sold in art supply stores. It handles much like white glue. You can choose a glossy (shiny) finish or a matte (dull) finish.

9

MEXICAN AND CENTRAL AMERICAN CRAFTS

Mexico is the southernmost country in North America. Central America lies between North and South America. Central America includes seven countries: Belize (buh-LEEZ), Guatemala (gwah-teh-MAH-luh), Honduras (hahn-DOO-russ), El Salvador (el SAL-vuh-door), Nicaragua (nih-kuh-RAH-gwah), Costa Rica (KOH-stuh REE-kuh), and Panama (PAN-uh-mah).

The Olmec (OHL-mek) people prospered in what is now southern Mexico from about 1500 B.C. to 100 B.C. The Olmecs carved huge figures from stone and sculpted smaller figures from clay.

Pottery, basketry, and cloth weaving were developed by the Mayans (MY-unz), who had a powerful empire in Central America from about A.D. 300 to 900. The Aztecs (AZZ-teks) ruled from about A.D. 900 to 1500. The Mayan and Aztec cultures spread south from Mexico to Central America.

In the 16th century, Spanish explorers conquered the region and converted many native people to Christianity. Eventually, craftspeople blended Indian and European designs into a style called Hispanic (hiss-PAN-ick).

Crafts throughout Mexico and Central America are made with similar methods. But styles may vary from village to village, because many people there cannot travel easily. Artisans do not always see what people in other villages are making, and they develop their own designs.

UNITED STATES

ATLANTIC

OCEAN

Gulf
of
Mexico

MEXICO

BELIZE

HONDURAS

GUATEMALA

NICARAGUA

EL SALVADOR

PACIFIC

OCEAN

COSTA RICA

PANAMA

Tin Ornaments

Color your ornaments with felt-tip pens. When the metal reflects light, the colors will look dazzling!

TIN CRAFTS

Bright red roosters, golden suns, and gleaming blue angels appear in many Mexican stores and markets. These ornaments are made from tin sheets, cut into shapes, and painted in brilliant colors.

Central American Indians were introduced to tinsmithing (creating objects from sheets of tin) by the Spanish. Lanterns, boxes, and other useful things are still created from tin.

TECHNIQUE

For a simple ornament, a tinsmith uses tin snips (scissors heavy enough to cut tin), to cut a flat tin sheet into an animal, angel, or other design. He or she then uses other tools to create a raised design on the ornament. This is called embossing. One stroke of a round punch makes a small dot on the tin's surface. Embossing a larger area—such as the body of a deer—requires repeated hammering.

For a more complex figure, such as a three-dimensional rocking horse, several tin pieces are bent and soldered (SAH-derd)—joined together with hot liquid metal that hardens when it cools.

Turning tin sheets into decorations began around 1920. Now a great variety of ornaments are made in different parts of Mexico.

HOW-TO PROJECT

You can make tin ornaments from disposable baking trays that are sold in supermarkets. Decorate your ornaments with permanent markers or acrylic paints.

Caution: The cut edges of baking trays may be sharp. Handle your ornaments carefully.

Also take care with your markers and paints. Clean brushes and wipe up any drips immediately.

You need:

Aluminum baking trays
  (disposable kind)
Markers, permanent type, or
  acrylic paints and brushes
Pencil
Ballpoint pen
Scissors (an old pair)
Paper punch
Tape
Several newspapers (to cover
  your work area)
Yarn or ribbon

1 With your scissors, cut away the sides from a baking tray. You now have a flat sheet of aluminum. Then photocopy or trace one of the patterns from page 17 of this book, or draw one of your own. Tape the pattern to the aluminum sheet.

2 Draw on top of the paper pattern with a pencil. Press firmly, tracing all the pattern's lines.

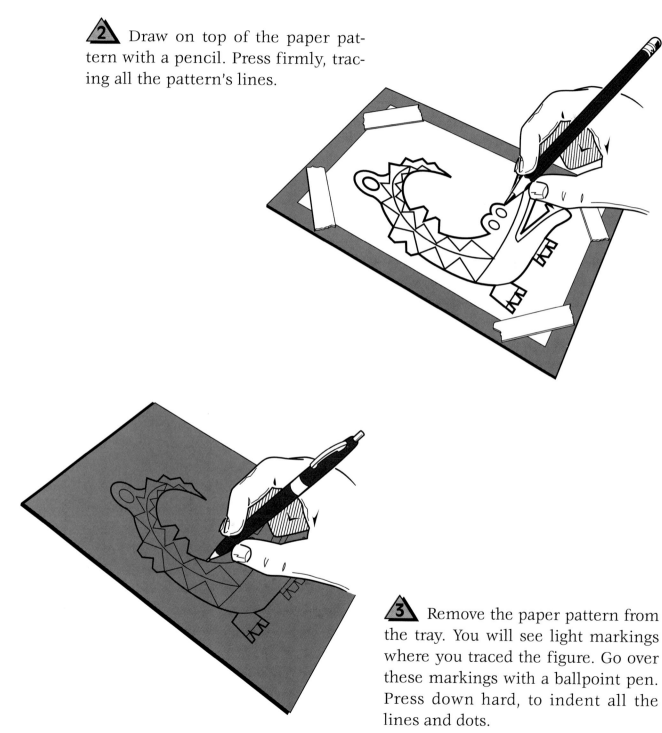

3 Remove the paper pattern from the tray. You will see light markings where you traced the figure. Go over these markings with a ballpoint pen. Press down hard, to indent all the lines and dots.

4 Cut out your ornament, along the outside line only. Then place the ornament so the pen marks are facing down. Color between the raised lines with markers or acrylic paint. Ornaments colored with markers can be covered with a finish. (See page 9 for more information about craft finishes.)

5 Using a paper punch, punch a hole in your ornament at the center top. Loop a piece of yarn or ribbon through the hole and tie it tightly.

WHAT ELSE YOU CAN DO

Create Your Own: When you design your own ornaments, draw simple outlines. Add details inside.

Greeting Cards: It's easy to send tin ornaments in the mail. You can even write simple messages on your tin cards. Your friends will like them! They're more than just cards—they're gifts.

Photocopy these designs to make patterns for your ornaments. You can copy them at the same size, or enlarge them with the photocopier. Cut patterns apart at the dotted lines.

Papel Picado

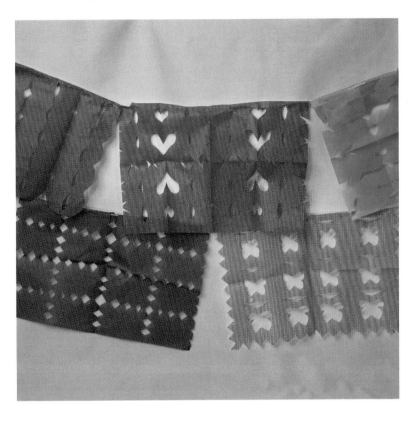

Colorful papel picado is glued to long pieces of string and stretched high across a street.

PAPEL PICADO

Papel picado (pah-PELL pee-KAH-doh) is a folk craft developed in Mexico. The paper originally used in papel picado was introduced to Mexico by the Spanish. In fact, papel picado means "pierced paper" in Spanish.

During the week before any national or local holiday, families—especially children—make tissue paper banners, place mats, and tablecloths. The banners often show patterns of birds and flowers.

TECHNIQUE

Papel picado is made by cutting shapes into a thin material, usually tissue paper. The paper is folded or stacked before it is cut, and when the layers are separated, a pattern is revealed.

Children cut their papel picado with scissors. But an expert paper cutter uses sharp chisel-like tools. First the cutter layers several unfolded sheets of paper on a board. Then the cutter hammers the tools so that their sharp edges cut through the pile of paper. The papers are sometimes folded in half first, resulting in a symmetrical picture—a picture that is identical on opposite sides.

A woman looks at papel picado in a Mexican marketplace. Papel picado is sometimes made from metallic foil or plastic sheeting. Designs sometimes show pictures of cowboys, dragons, or skeletons playing guitars.

HOW-TO PROJECT

A sheet of tissue paper is usually 30 inches by 20 inches. When cut into quarters, your tissue paper will be the size of Mexican papel, which measures 15 by 10 inches.

> **You need:**
>
> Tissue paper sheets, cut into quarters
> Scissors

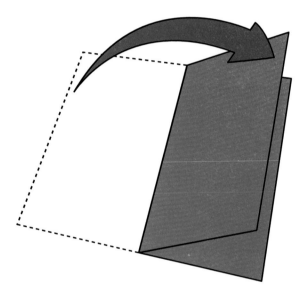

1 Fold a piece of tissue paper in half the short way.

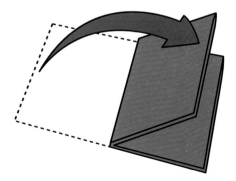

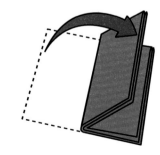

2 Fold the tissue paper in half two more times.

3 Cut away sections from the folded edges. Do not cut all the way from one edge to the opposite edge. If you do, the paper will fall apart. Carefully unfold the paper.

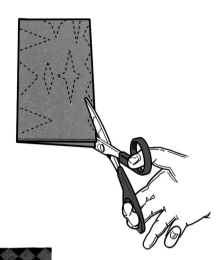

WHAT ELSE YOU CAN DO

Papel Banners: For a birthday party, or any other celebration, make papel picado banners. Tie a long piece of string between two chairs. Fold one long edge of each papel over the string. Glue down the folded edge, or staple it just below the string. Raise the banner high and tape it between two walls or trees with masking tape. (First make sure that the tape will not damage the walls.)

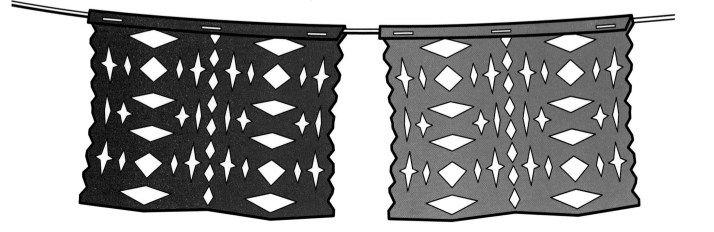

Guatemalan Weaving

With yarn and drinking straws, you can make a brightly patterned belt.

GUATEMALAN WEAVING

Guatemalan clothes and blankets are well known for their vivid colors. Fabrics are woven by hand from wool or cotton. The colors and patterns are based on Mayan designs, some of which are hundreds of years old. Many Guatemalan Indians wear traditional, handwoven clothing. Women often wear a skirt, a bulky headdress, and an overblouse called a *huipil* (HWEE-peel). The garments are held together with a sash around the waist.

Most Guatemalans live in the mountains that extend east to west across the country. About three-quarters of all Guatemalans are Indians. They speak Indian languages and wear traditional Indian clothing.

TECHNIQUE

Guatemalan women weave narrow strips of fabric on looms called backstraps, which are very similar to those used by ancient Mayans. One end of the loom is tied around a tree and the other end around the weaver's body. The weaver sits just the right distance from the tree to keep the yarn pulled tight. Once completed, several strips are sewn together to make larger pieces of cloth.

Guatemalan men are weavers, too. They weave wider pieces of cloth by standing or sitting at larger looms, called treadles. These wider pieces of cloth are often made into skirts.

The patterns a weaver chooses depend on where the weaver lives. Designs vary from village to village, and they are handed down through generations.

These Guatemalan women wear embroidered huipils. Typical designs might include stripes and zigzags, bright yellow birds, or deep purple flowers.

HOW-TO PROJECT

You can weave a belt of any length on a loom made from drinking straws.

You need:

4 plastic drinking straws
1 skein of 4-ply yarn
Scissors
Tape measure

1 Cut 4 pieces of yarn, each 80 inches long. Cut ½ inch off the end of a drinking straw. Slide the small piece to the middle of one of the pieces of yarn.

2 Now pull both ends of the yarn through one of the long pieces of straw. Sucking on the straw end helps pull the yarn through. Cut and thread the other 3 straws the same way.

3 Gather the ends of the yarn together and tie them in a loose knot.

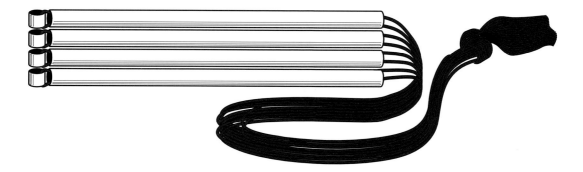

4 Knot the end of the yarn on the skein to one straw. Weave the yarn between each of the 4 straws, winding the yarn under one straw and over the next.

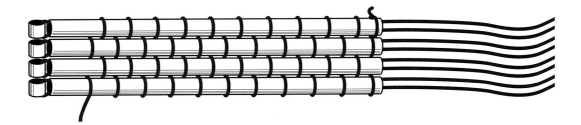

5 Once you have woven about 3 to 4 inches, push the woven yarn off the straws. Continue weaving and pushing the work off the straws until you run out of room to push the weaving off the straws.

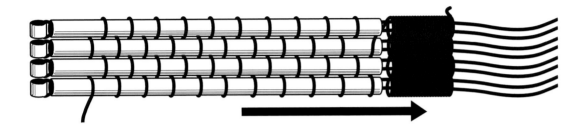

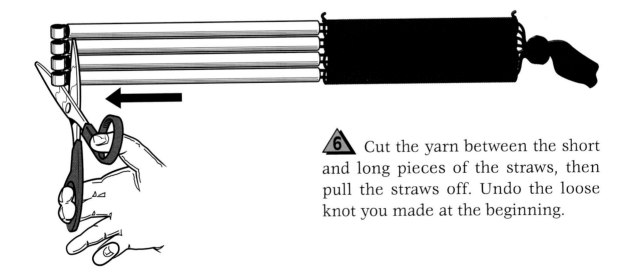

6 Cut the yarn between the short and long pieces of the straws, then pull the straws off. Undo the loose knot you made at the beginning.

7 Tie both ends of the belt into tight knots. Leave fringes of yarn several inches long below the knots. Trim off any extra.

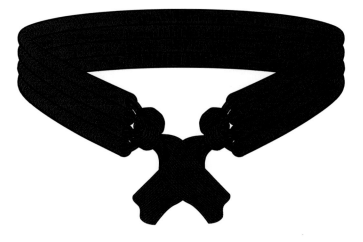

WHAT ELSE YOU CAN DO

Other Sizes: The above directions produce a belt for waist sizes up to 32 inches. Cut yarn longer or shorter for other waist sizes.

Variations: Braid the yarn ends for a different kind of fringe. Or sew on snaps to make the belt fit your waist. Use variegated yarn for a belt of many colors.

Group Project: Sew several belts together to make a rug. Or you can sew several shorter belts together to make a place mat.

Otomi Paper Figures

A brown paper bag— crushed and flattened— imitates the rough paper that Mexicans call amate.

AMATE PAPER

The Mayans are believed to have developed the rough-textured paper known as amate (ah-MAH-tay) more than 1,000 years ago. The Otomi Indians of a village called San Pablito are the only people who still make amate.

The Otomi cut the paper into animal and human figures. The figures represent spirits that can bring good or bad luck. Medium-brown paper figures are

The Otomi Indians live in San Pablito, Mexico, a small mountain village northeast of Mexico City. They make amate from the bark of fig trees. To keep the trees from becoming extinct, the Otomi plant 10 trees for every tree cut down for papermaking.

prepared for sick people to fight illness. Light colors are used for love charms, or to ensure a large crop.

The Otomi also send amate from San Pablito to other parts of Mexico. Artisans paint amate with colorful birds, flowers, and scenes of everyday life.

TECHNIQUE

Otomi men cut long, narrow strips of bark from amate trees. Otomi women finish the papermaking process. First the women boil the amate bark to soften it. Next they layer the boiled bark on a wooden board. Then they pound the strips with a stone until the fibers bind together into a sturdy sheet.

Each sheet is folded in half lengthwise before it is cut into a figure. When the paper is unfolded, the figure is symmetrical. The figures can vary in size, but most amate paper figures are about eight inches long.

Some Mexican artisans use amate paper as a surface for painting. Figures and paintings made from amate are sold as souvenirs and wall decorations.

HOW-TO PROJECT

The patterns on page 56 show typical magic figures made from amate paper. You can copy one of them or invent your own.

You need:

Brown shopping bags
  or brown wrapping paper
Pencil or marker
Scissors

1 From one of the paper bags, cut a rectangle. It should measure about 8 inches by 10 inches. Crumple the paper tightly into a ball.

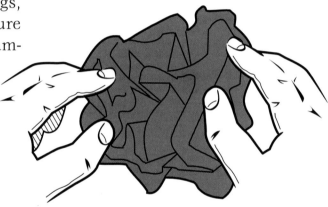

2 Uncrumple and flatten the paper, smoothing it with your hand. It will still be crinkly. Repeat crumpling and smoothing two or three times.

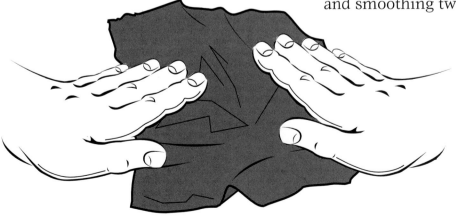

3 Fold the paper in half. Imagining the fold as the figure's center, draw half a figure against the folded edge.

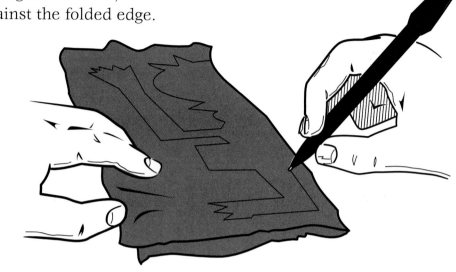

4 Cut on the outline, then open the paper flat.

WHAT ELSE YOU CAN DO

Greeting Cards: Glue paper figures to pieces of folded construction paper or stationery. Use just a little glue in several spots. Draw faces and clothing on your figures, if you like.

Day of the Dead Skeleton

Day of the Dead skeletons can look scary or full of fun. Decorate them with glitter, sequins, and whatever else you can think of!

DAY OF THE DEAD

Each November 2—All Souls' Day—people all over Mexico celebrate the Day of the Dead, or *el Dio de los Muertos* (ell DEE-oh deh lohs moo-AIR-tohs). Families visit cemeteries, where they clean the graves, spread them with flowers, and offer dead relatives their favorite foods. In homes, families decorate altars with flowers, candles, and photos.

El Dio de los Muertos is not a grim day at all, but a time for the living to celebrate and remember the dead. Figures of skeletons and grinning skulls can be seen everywhere. Papier-mâché skeletons decorate store windows. Some skeletons are shown dancing the popular Mexican Hat Dance, while others ride on bicycles or are laid out in coffins. Children buy special skull-shaped sugar candies. Bakers make a bread called *pan de muertos* (PAHN deh moo-AIR-tohs), or bread of the dead. They decorate the bread with bones made from frosting. Bakers also put small sugar skeletons and chocolate skulls on top of cakes.

Cardboard and papier-mâché skeletons come out for the Day of the Dead.

HOW-TO PROJECT

Children in Mexico often make cardboard skeletons for the Day of the Dead. You can make your own cardboard skeleton with moveable arms and legs.

You need:

White cardboard or poster board
White paper
8 double-pronged paper fasteners
Black and red markers
Pencil
Scissors
Rubber band
Tape
Sequins
Glitter
Glue

1 With a pencil and white paper, trace the 10 skeleton pieces printed on page 35. (Or copy the pieces with a photocopier. You can make them the same size, or you can make them larger.) Cut out the pieces.

2 Place the paper patterns on white cardboard or poster board. Trace around the pieces with a pencil and draw on the small circles.

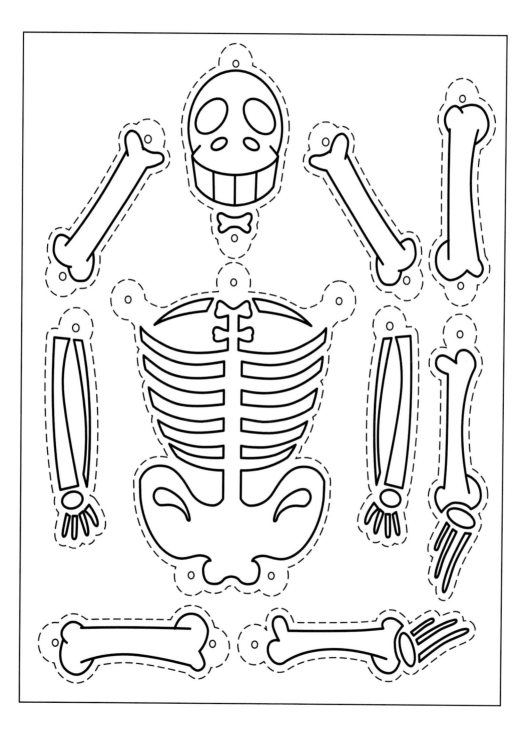

3 Draw bones on the pieces with a black marker. Add other features with a red marker. Cut out the pieces.

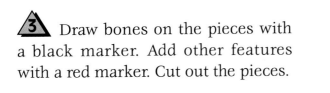

4 Punch holes through the small circles with a paper punch.

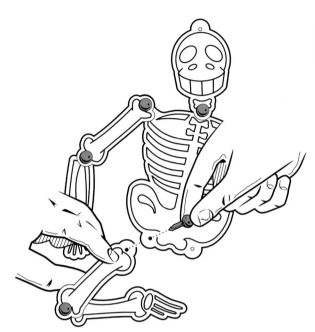

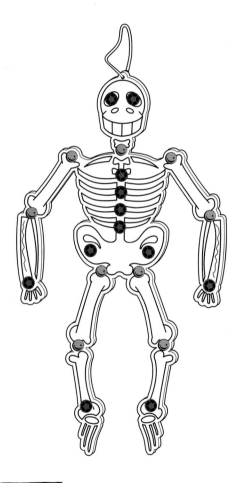

5 Attach the skeleton's arms and legs behind the body with paper fasteners. If the arms and legs do not move easily, loosen the fasteners.

6 Glue sequins and glitter onto your skeleton, wherever you like. Tape a rubber band behind the head. When you hold the rubber band, you can wiggle the skeleton so that its arms and legs move.

WHAT ELSE YOU CAN DO

Clothing: Make a hat or other clothing for your skeleton from paper or cloth. Attach the pieces to the cardboard with a few drops of white glue.

Door Decoration: Make a larger (5-foot) skeleton to hang on a door for Halloween.

Tree of Life

You can make a colorful Tree of Life from self-hardening clay (right) or oven-bake clay (left)

TREES OF LIFE

A Tree of Life is an elaborately decorated clay candleholder. In Mexican homes, Trees of Life are lit on religious holidays. Very large Trees of Life are often carried in festival processions.

Trees of Life were first made by Indians after Spanish explorers arrived in Mexico. Traditionally, the decorations on the candlesticks represent biblical stories such as Adam and Eve in the Garden of Eden. Yet, Trees of Life are often decorated with many other patterns and figures.

TECHNIQUE

Trees of Life vary in size from six inches to six feet high. Sculptors form the Trees of Life from sandy clay. They work mainly with their hands, but sometimes they use tools. They may use a stick for smoothing the clay, or a piece of wire to cut off extra clay. Some sculptors press the clay into prepared molds.

The sculptor forms the tree trunk first, then adds branches on both sides. Small clay decorations are attached next. When the clay is dry, the tree may be painted in many colors. Younger family members may help to shape and attach the clay decorations or paint the tree.

Mexican Trees of Life are often quite complex, decorated with clay fruits, flowers, or figures representing biblical stories.

HOW-TO PROJECT

Clay: For making Trees of Life, use a clay that hardens when it dries. (Do not use modeling clays, which do not harden.) Some clays harden by drying in the open air. Other clays must dry in a heated oven. If you choose a clay that has to be baked, make sure the baking can be done in a home oven. Whichever kind of clay you use, *always follow the directions on the package.*

Work Surface: Cover your work surface with newspaper. Tape down the newspaper with masking tape. Then lay down a small piece of plastic wrap on top.

Roll your clay on the newspaper and build your Tree of Life on the plastic wrap. You can turn your tree on the plastic while you work, and the tree will be easy to move when you are done.

Joining Pieces Together: Always join pieces of clay with water. Pieces that are not moistened will separate when drying.

First wet the two pieces where they are to be joined. Press the pieces together, then smooth the outside of the joint with your moistened fingertips. Smooth hard-to-reach places with the side of a toothpick. You may also add tiny bits of clay to smooth over a joint. Just remember to keep the clay and your fingers moist.

You need:

Self-hardening or oven-bake
  clay
Tempera or acrylic paints
Several newspapers
Masking tape
Plastic wrap
Paper towels
Ruler
Bowl of water
Toothpicks or wire
Candle

1 Roll a lump of clay into a ball that measures about 2 inches across. Press the clay ball on a piece of plastic wrap, flattening the bottom. This is the base of the tree.

2 For the tree trunk, roll a lump of clay into a sausage that measures about 4 inches long and ¾ inch thick. Flatten the ends with your moistened finger.

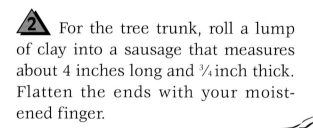

3 Join one end of the trunk to the center of the base. The trunk may bend, depending on the kind of clay you use. If this happens, push one or two toothpicks or a piece of wire down the middle of the trunk to keep it straight.

4 For each branch, roll a clay sausage about 4½ inches long and ½ inch thick. Flatten the ends with your moistened finger. Bend the branches to form two half circles. Join the branches to the trunk, as shown in the illustration.

5 Roll another lump of clay into a 1-inch ball. Poke a toothpick into one side and twirl it, forming a hollow big enough to hold a candle. Attach the candleholder to the top of the tree's trunk.

6 Wet your finger and smooth the whole surface of the Tree of Life. Shape birds, flowers, or small balls of clay and attach them to the branches. Put the tree in an out-of-the-way place to dry for a day or two. Or bake your tree as directed on the package of clay. When your tree is completely dry, paint it in bright colors.

WHAT ELSE YOU CAN DO

Indents: While the clay is still moist, scratch patterns in your tree with a toothpick or fork. Try making stripes, dots, or other geometric patterns.

Markers and Crayons: Try using these instead of paint. They work on some clays.

Celebrations: Make Trees of Life for gifts. Or use them as party decorations for birthdays, Valentine's Day (add lots of red hearts to your trees), and other occasions. For a special celebration, make a large Tree of Life. You may have to insert pieces of wire into the tree trunk and branches for added support.

Art Clay: Oven-bake art clay is especially easy to handle, and it comes in many different colors. Fimo and Sculpey are two popular brands that are sold in art supply stores. When using this type of clay, follow the special directions on the package.

Guatemalan Worry Dolls

Using wire twist-ties as a base, you can make tiny dolls called worry dolls.

WORRY DOLLS

In Guatemala dolls are made from scrap materials. Some tiny dolls are called worry dolls or trouble dolls. Children may take them to bed with them at night. Before the children fall asleep, they tell their worries to the dolls, one at a time. It is believed that the dolls take away the problems while the children sleep. Traditionally, about six dolls are kept together in a tiny wooden box.

Coffee, bananas, cotton, and sugar are important crops in Guatemala, where many people farm for a living. In the country's thick forests, Guatemalans harvest mahogany, a dark hardwood used to make furniture.

TECHNIQUE

Worry dolls are only about 1¼ inches tall. Some are even smaller. Each tiny doll is made from small pieces of wire, which are bent and twisted together to shape a body. Thin strips of paper are wound around the wire. The doll's clothing is made from yarn or small scraps of cloth and glued onto the paper. The paper on the doll's head is not covered so that a face can be drawn on it.

Dolls of all different sizes can be found in Guatemalan open-air markets, along with woven and embroidered cloth.

HOW-TO PROJECT ▰▰▰▰

Make your own worry dolls with wire twist-ties from the supermarket.

You need:

2 or 3 wire twist-ties, 4 inches long
Colored embroidery thread, yarn, or string
Scraps of colored paper
Scissors
Glue
Black marker

---

1 For a 3-inch doll, use 3 twist-ties. Twist 2 of the ties together, about 1 inch from the ends. Keep the short ends together for the doll's head, but separate the long ends for the doll's legs.

2 Wind the third twist-tie around for the doll's arms. Cut the ends so that the arms are even lengths. Bend the hands and feet.

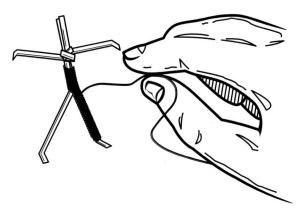

3 For a smaller doll, use 2 twist-ties. Fold 1 twist-tie in half for the doll's body. Separate the ends. Halfway up, twist them around.

4 Fold a second twist-tie in half. Twist it around the doll's body to form arms. Bend the wires to make hands and feet.

5 Either size doll will be finished the same way:

Knot a piece of thread to the wires where they cross, but leave a piece hanging. Wind the thread around the body and down one leg. Then wind the thread back up the leg.

Wind the thread down and up the other leg the same way. Knot the thread to the piece left hanging. Trim the ends close to the knot.

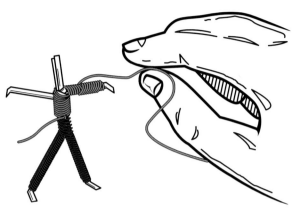

▲**6** With another color of thread, tie a knot around the doll's waist. Wrap the chest and wrap down and up the doll's arms in the same way that you wrapped the legs.

Crisscross the thread over the chest. To finish, cut the thread and glue the end to the doll's back.

▲**7** Cut a colored paper rectangle a little larger than the head. Fold the paper in half to make a square and snip off the lower corners.

⚠️ 8 Glue the paper around the doll's head. Draw a face on the front of it.

WHAT ELSE YOU CAN DO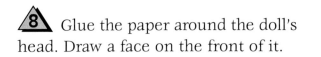

Other Clothing: Glue bits of fabric or ribbon onto the bodies to dress the dolls. Try making a skirt, hat, or head scarf.

Gifts: Guatemalan people often attach worry dolls to barrettes, belts, and wire wreaths. Try gluing your dolls to a barrette or attaching loops to them to make hanging ornaments. Or, decorate a small box to hold a set of worry dolls. Give it as a gift.

Cuna Molas

Make your mola from cloth (bottom and left) or craft paper (right).

MOLAS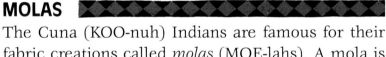

The Cuna (KOO-nuh) Indians are famous for their fabric creations called *molas* (MOE-lahs). A mola is a cloth rectangle stitched with pictures.

Mola designs often feature animals. Other common designs are based on myths and religious symbols. But designs may include a variety of subjects. Some mola designs are used only in certain Cuna villages.

Cuna women stitch molas to the front and back of puffy-sleeved blouses, which they wear every day. A Cuna girl learns to sew small molas when she is about seven years old. She is expected to become an expert as she grows older.

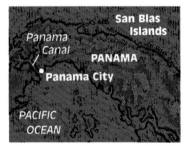

The Cuna Indians live on the San Blas Islands off the coast of Panama. They sometimes travel from island to island in dugout canoes. The Cuna choose to live separately from other Central American peoples, and making crafts with traditional methods is important to their way of life.

TECHNIQUE

Molas are created with a type of needlework called reverse appliqué (app-luh-KAY). Each mola is usually made of two to seven layers of cotton rectangles in different colors. The top layer is usually red to contrast with the bottom layer of black. The layers in between are often bright yellow, green, blue, and orange.

The Cuna woman begins her needlework by sewing together the edges of the layered cotton rectangles. She cuts away a shape from the top piece. She folds under the raw edges and stitches them down. Then she cuts into the next piece of fabric, revealing another layer of color. She repeats this process until a narrow strip of each layer appears.

Cuna women display their molas. Complicated molas may take several months to complete.

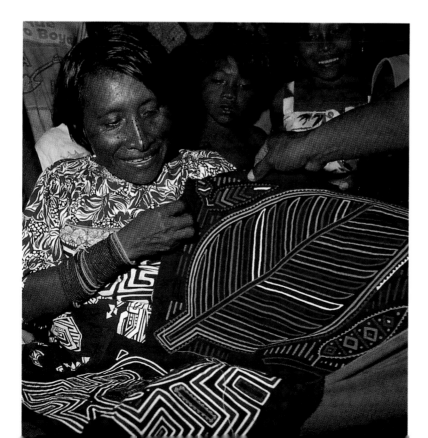

HOW-TO PROJECT

Sewing a mola from fabric is quite difficult, but you can achieve the same colorful effect with felt. Use the patterns shown in this book, or create your own designs. Make sure that your outlines are simple. You will cut each piece a little smaller than the one before it. The smaller certain shapes become, the harder they will be to cut.

> ***You need:***
>
> **Felt rectangles in red, yellow, and black**
> **Sheet of white paper**
> **Pencil**
> **Scissors**
> **Paper clips**
> **White glue**

1 Trace the pattern below onto a sheet of paper, or photocopy it. Do not cut it out. There are more mola patterns on page 57.

2 Place a red piece of felt on top of a yellow piece. Place the paper pattern on top of the felt and clip the paper and felt together.

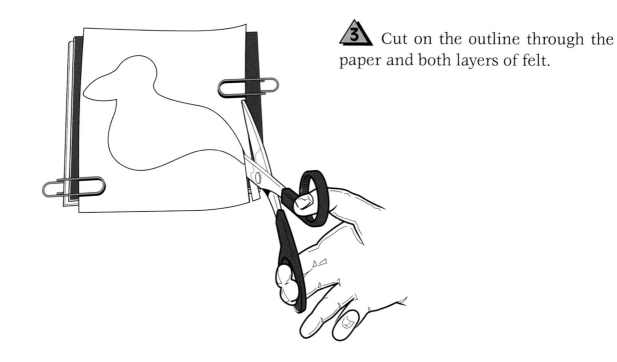

3 Cut on the outline through the paper and both layers of felt.

4 Separate the paper and the 2 pieces of felt. Draw a new outline on your paper pattern, ¼ inch from the paper's edges.

5 Clip the pattern to the red felt shape and cut on the new outline.

6 Glue the red shape on top of the yellow shape. You need just a few drops of glue in several places. Glue the layered shapes to a piece of black felt.

▲ Add detail to your mola. Cut other small shapes from felt and glue them on top of your design and around it.

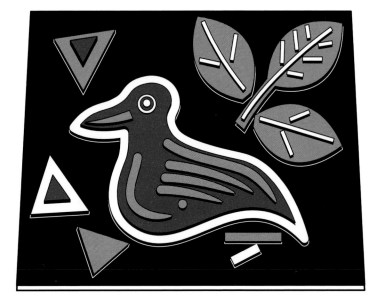

WHAT ELSE YOU CAN DO

More Layers: After you have practiced with a 2-layer mola, try cutting a pattern from 3 or 4 layers. Make each layer a different color.

Paper Molas: Use construction paper or other colored art papers instead of felt.

Invitations: If you have made an especially beautiful mola, photocopy it in color for party invitations.

MORE PATTERNS

Trace or photocopy these patterns. The Otomi paper figures project starts on page 30.
The Cuna molas project starts on page 52.

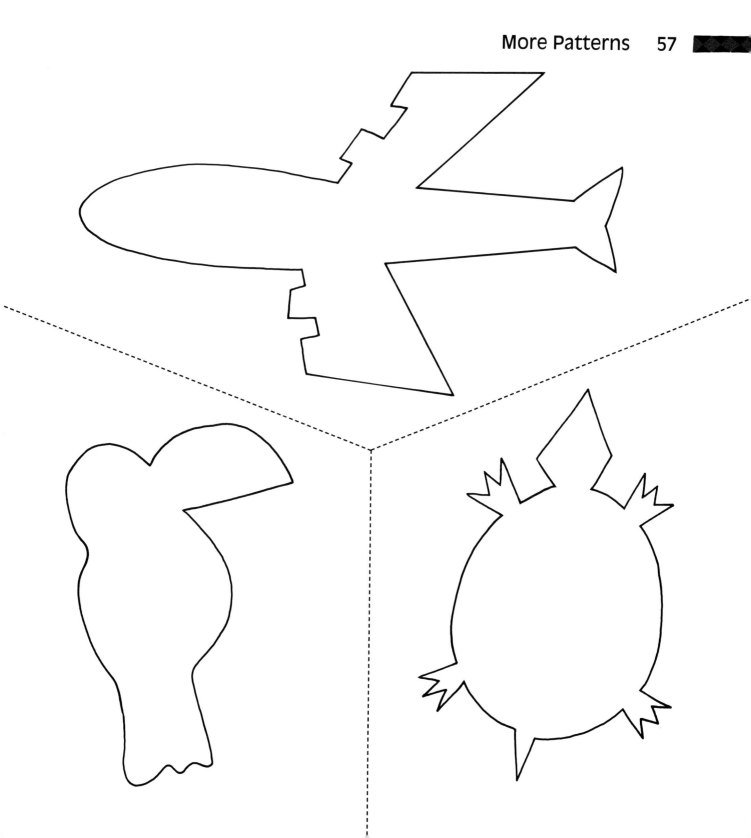

METRIC CONVERSION CHART

If you want to use the metric system, convert measurements using the chart on the right. Because fractions can be hard to work with, round all metric measurements to the nearest whole number.

when you know:	multiply by:	to find:
Length		
inches	25.00	millimeters
inches	2.54	centimeters
feet	30.00	centimeters
feet	.30	meters
yards	.91	meters
miles	1.61	kilometers
Volume		
teaspoons	5.00	milliliters
tablespoons	15.00	milliliters
fluid ounces	30.00	milliliters
cups	0.24	liters
pints	0.47	liters
quarts	0.95	liters
gallons	3.80	liters
Weight		
ounces	28.00	grams
pounds	0.45	kilograms

GLOSSARY

amate: A rough textured paper that is made from the bark of fig trees

appliqué: A fabric cutout put on a larger piece of material for decoration, *or* a type of needlework in which appliqués are used

artisan: A person who is very skilled at making crafts

culture: The customs, ideas, and traditions of a certain group of people. Culture includes religious celebrations, arts and crafts, folktales, costumes, and food.

Day of the Dead: A holiday in which people celebrate the lives of deceased family members and friends. In Mexico it is called *el Dio de los Muertos.*

emboss: To decorate a surface with a raised design

geometric patterns: Patterns that use simple shapes, such as circles, triangles, or squares

huipil: A handwoven overblouse that is part of the traditional Guatemalan woman's dress

Mayans: American Indian people who developed a great civilization in what is now Central America. The Mayans' powerful empire lasted from about A.D. 300 to 900.

molas: Cloth rectangles stitched with pictures. Molas are created with a type of needlework called reverse appliqué. The craft originated with the Cuna Indians.

papel picado: A folk craft developed in Mexico, in which elaborate patterns are cut into paper. Papel picado means "pierced paper" in Spanish.

solder: To join metal pieces together with hot liquid metal that hardens when it cools

symmetrical: Appearing the same on opposite sides

tinsmith: A person who creates objects from sheets of tin

READ MORE ABOUT MEXICO AND CENTRAL AMERICA

Fiction & Folktales

Bierhorst, John, ed. *The Monkey's Haircut and Other Stories Told by the Maya,* illustrations by Robert Andrew Parker. New York: William Morrow, 1986.

Cameron, Ann. *The Most Beautiful Place in the World,* illustrations by Thomas B. Allen. New York: Alfred A. Knopf, 1988.

Castañeda, Omar S. *Abuela's Weave,* illustrations by Enrique O. Sanchez. New York: Lee & Low, 1993.

Czernecki, Stefan and Timothy Rhodes. *The Hummingbirds' Gift,* illustrations by Stefan Czernecki. New York: Hyperion Books for Children, 1994.

Gerson, Mary-Joan. *People of Corn: A Mayan Story,* illustrations by Carla Golembe. Boston: Little, Brown, 1995.

Head, Judith. *Culebra Cut.* Minneapolis: Carolrhoda Books, 1995.

Lattimore, Deborah Nourse. *The Flame of Peace: A Tale of the Aztecs,* illustrations by the author. New York: Harper & Row, 1987.

Stevens, Jan Romero. *Carlos and the Squash Plant,* illustrations by Jeanne Arnold. Flagstaff, AZ: Northland, 1993.

Volkmer, Jane Anne. *Song of the Chirimía/La Música de la Chirimía,* illustrations by the author. Minneapolis: Carolrhoda Books, 1990.

Nonfiction

Ancona, George. *Pablo Remembers: The Fiesta of the Day of the Dead,* photographs by the author. New York: Lothrop, Lee and Shepard, 1993.

Ancona, George. *The Piñata Maker/El Piñatero,* photographs by the author. San Diego: Harcourt, 1994.

Goldstein, Ernest. *The Journey of Diego Rivera.* Minneapolis: Lerner Publications, 1995.

Haskins, Jim. *Count Your Way through Mexico,* illustrations by Helen Byers. Minneapolis: Carolrhoda Books, 1989.

Lasky, Kathryn. *Days of the Dead,* photographs by Christopher B. Knight. New York: Hyperion Books for Children, 1994.

Matthews, Sally Schafer. *The Sad Night: The Story of an Aztec Victory and a Spanish Loss,* illustrations by the author. New York: Clarion Books, 1994.

Staub, Frank. *The Children of the Sierra Madre,* photographs by the author. Minneapolis: Carolrhoda Books, 1996.

Staub, Frank. *Children of Yucatán,* photographs by the author. Minneapolis: Carolrhoda Books, 1996.

Winter, Jonah. *Diego,* illustrations by Jeanette Winter. New York: Knopf, 1991.

Wolf, Bernard. *Beneath the Stone: A Mexican Zapotec Tale.* New York: Orchard Books, 1994.

INDEX

ABOUT THE AUTHOR

Florence Temko is an internationally known author of more than 30 books on world folkcrafts and paper arts. She has traveled in 31 countries, gaining much of her skill firsthand. Ms. Temko shows her enthusiasm for crafts through simple, inventive adaptations of traditional arts and crafts projects. She has presented hundreds of hands-on programs in schools and museums, including the Metropolitan Museum of Art in New York City, and at many education conferences across the country. She lives in San Diego, California.

ACKNOWLEDGMENTS

The photographs in this book are reproduced with the permission of:

p. 6 (left), Turkish Republic, Ministry of Culture and Tourism; p. 6 (right), Wilford Archaeology Laboratory, University of Minnesota, by Kathy Raskob/IPS; p. 7 (left), Nelson-Atkins Museum of Art, Kansas City, Missouri (Purchase: Nelson Trust); p. 7 (right), Freer Gallery of Art, Smithsonian Institution; pp. 8, 9, 12, 18, 22, 28, 32, 38, 44, 50, Robert L. and Diane Wolfe; pp. 13 (both), 19, 33 (right), 51 (left), © Gary Retherford; pp. 23, 51 (right), © Suzanne L. Murphy; p. 29, © J. P. Couran, DDB Stock Photo; p. 33 (left), © Alyx Kellington 1992, DDB Stock Photo; p. 39, © Bazaar del Mundo, Old Town, San Diego; p. 45, © D. Donne Bryant, DDB Stock Photo.

The maps and illustrations on pages 2, 10-11, 22, 28, 44, 50, 56, and 57 are by John Erste.